Working Iron

in

Merthyr Tydfil

Richard Hayman

MERTHYR TYDFIL HERITAGE TRUST

Dowlais Works and town in 1875.

The cover shows a view of Dowlais Ironworks, painted by G. Childs in 1840.

Preface

No other natural element has had so profound an effect on our material civilisation as iron. The success of the iron trade in the eighteenth and nineteenth centuries was the momentum behind the Industrial Revolution that enabled Britain to achieve its world power status, and keep ahead of its rivals in the technological race. Brunel's Great Western Railway and Clifton Suspension Bridge, Stephenson's Rocket, and Paxton's Crystal Palace are among the more spectacular examples, mass produced chain, nuts and bolts and tin cans among the more mundane—these are just a few of the innovations that would not have been possible without iron.

Throughout the Industrial Revolution the British iron industry was concentrated in a few small geographical areas, and by the early nineteenth century was dominated by the ironworks in South Wales and Staffordshire. The most important centre of production in South Wales was Merthyr Tydfil where the Dowlais works had been founded in 1759, to be followed by Plymouth in 1763, Cyfarthfa in 1765 and Penydarren in 1784. Two of these works, Cyfarthfa and Dowlais, were later to enjoy the, albeit shortlived, status of being the largest ironworks in the world.

When B. H. Malkin visited Merthyr in 1803 he wrote: 'When the first furnaces and forges were erected, there could not have been the slightest glimmering of prescience, that this little obscure Welsh village would, in less than forty years, grow up to such a magnitude, as to be far more populous than any other town in Wales.' In 1801 Merthyr Tydfil already had a population of nearly 8,000, and had overtaken Swansea to become the largest town in Wales. However even Malkin could not have forseen how the town's population would continue to grow rapidly over the next fifty years as the boom in the demand for iron products gathered pace. In 1851 Merthyr had a population of 46,000 people, nearly half of whom were directly employed in the iron industry or its collieries. Throughout this period Merthyr kept its pre-eminent position as the nation's leading iron producing town, specialising in the manufacture of high quality rails which were exported to railway companies as far afield as Germany, Russia, India and the USA.

The history of Merthyr's iron industry is also to a large extent the history of its people. The meteoric rise of the industry had two consequences that were perhaps inevitable—fortunes were made and squalor was created. Living conditions in nineteenth century Merthyr were as bad as they were in Victorian Liverpool and Manchester. Social tensions were ever present, provoking riots in 1800, 1816 and 1831, the consequence of which was a military garrison permanently stationed in the town. When the iron industry went into terminal decline in the latter half of the nineteenth century its workforce were increasingly drawn toward radical politics, and so it is no surprise to learn that Merthyr Tydfil returned Keir Hardie to Westminster in 1900 as Britain's first Labour MP. Merthyr survived the closure of its ironworks by switching its economic base to coal mining. Nevertheless the phenomenal growth of the iron industry has given Merthyr Tydfil one of the most extraordinary histories of any British town.

The Technology of the Iron Industry

Iron has been one of the most useful elements known to man for the last 4,000 years. In prehistory it was produced in small clay hearths by heating iron rich ore with charcoal. The basic principle of this technique is still applicable today. Iron has a strong chemical attraction to oxygen and is found in the form of iron oxide, so the way to remove it is to heat it in the presence of carbon. Carbon has an even stronger attraction to oxygen and unites with it to form carbon monoxide, leaving the iron in its pure state. In the early hearths, known as bloomeries, small pieces of iron, or blooms, would form after several hours of heating, which could then be hammered to form tools or weapons.

This technique remained the only way of producing iron until the *blast furnace* was invented near Liege in Belgium in about 1400 AD. The early blast furnaces were masonry structures about 10-12ft in height, lined with firebricks. Iron ore and charcoal were loaded into the top of the furnace, known as *charging*, which was kept constantly heated by blowing air into the base by means of pipes known as *tuyeres*. To provide this constant *blast* of air mechanical bellows or cylinders operated by a waterwheel were used. Unlike the bloomery the blast furnace produced molten iron which formed at the base, or hearth, of the furnace and was allowed to run out, or be *tapped*, by unblocking a clay taphole. The molten iron was allowed to run out into beds of sand moulded in such a way as to allow the iron to solidify in blocks of manageable size. The blast furnace enabled as much as a ton of iron to be produced in 24 hours, compared to the few pounds that could be produced in the bloomery.

The iron produced by the blast furnace was known as *pig iron*. In the early years it was sometimes moulded to form such items as cannons, firebacks and domestic utensils. However usually it was re-melted to remove some of its impurities to form what is properly termed cast iron. This is basically iron which has a carbon content of 3-4 per cent. It has a crystalline structure, and is strong in compression—which made it important in structural engineering—and was made by pouring it in its molten state into moulds.

A—Furnace. B—Stairs. C—Ore. D—Charcoal.

A typical early blast furnace, taken from Georgius Agricola's De Re Metallica, *published in Germany in 1556.*

The more common form of iron was wrought iron, which contains virtually no impurities. It has a fibrous structure and when heated can be rolled or hammered

A puddling furnace at Cwmbran, showing the puddler about to remove a ball of semi-molten iron.

to the required shape. It is also much more resistant to corrosion than the mild steel that replaced it, although more expensive to produce. Its production involved refining pig iron in two stages. The first stage was the *finery*, which was little different to the earlier bloomery, where the iron was stirred until it formed a spongy mass, and then cast into water cooled blocks before being sent to the *chafery*. Here the iron was heated only until it became malleable, when it was removed and hammered to its finished shape. This repeated hammering was necessary because it allowed the impurities in the iron, known as *slag*, to be beaten out.

The further technological breakthroughs that allowed the iron industry to expand rapidly came in the eighteenth century. Blast furnaces consumed vast quantities of charcoal which resulted in the depletion of the nation's reserves of trees. Several attempts were made to use coal instead, but these were unsuccessful because the sulphur in coal contaminates the iron. But in 1709 Abraham Darby, at his works in Coalbrookdale, Shropshire, had the ingenious idea of smelting iron using coke, which he produced by burning coal in the same way that charcoal was made. The results were highly successful, and proved much more effective than the

A sketch by J. M. W. Turner made in the 1790s of an unidentified ironworks showing a water powered shingling hammer.

charcoal furnace. Although the new process was slow to catch on initially, by the end of the eighteenth century the charcoal furnace was obsolete.

The early eighteenth century also saw the introduction of the rolling mill, whereby wrought iron could be shaped mechanically rather than having to be hammered. However the problem remained of finding a simpler method of converting pig to wrought iron than the laborious and time consuming finery and chafery. Several experiments in this field were carried out, for example by the Cranage brothers at Coalbrookdale in the 1760s. Peter Onions, working at Dowlais, patented a process in 1783, but he specified that the iron should be hammered rather than rolled, which is the most likely reason why it failed to be adopted. The process which the iron trade did adopt was known as *puddling*,

In this view of Cyfarthfa, drawn in about 1800 by William Pamplin, the layout of the works is clearly seen. In the background coal is being converted in open heaps to coke. The furnaces, powered by a 48ft diameter waterwheel, are to the left. Above them are the charging houses, and below them are the casting sheds where the molten iron was allowed to run out into the pig beds. The large building to the right, with its numerous chimneys, housed the puddling furnaces and rolling mills.

and was patented in 1784 by Henry Cort of Fontley in Hampshire. He used a special reverberatory furnace in which coal was burnt in a firebox and the hot gases were drawn across a separate compartment containing the pig iron. By keeping the coal and iron apart sulphur was prevented from contaminating the iron. The iron was stirred by the puddler to allow it to mix with air, the result of which was that the carbon reacted with oxygen to form carbon monoxide. This left a spongy mass of wrought iron which was then hammered in order to remove the slag, and to shape it ready for the rolling mill.

The coke fired blast furnace and the puddling process were the two stages of ironmaking employed in Merthyr Tydfil, and although the processes were improved and modified throughout the early nineteenth century the basic principles remained the same. Merthyr Tydfil was particularly well situated for the establishment of iron works. At the northern edge of the South Wales coalfield it had excellent reserves of coal and ironstone which were found on or near the surface, making it easy and cheap to exploit. Limestone, which was needed only in small quantities as a flux in the blast furnace, could be quarried from the north side of the town. Also the river Taff and the Morlais Brook provided the plentiful water supply which in the early years was essential for the operation of the waterwheels that powered the blowing cylinders and drove the machinery.

The Growth of Merthyr's Iron Industry

Ironworking began in Merthyr Tydfil in the Elizabethan period. Throughout the sixteenth century most of Britain's iron had come from the Weald in Sussex, but the demand for large quantities of charcoal led to a decline in woodland to the extent that legislation was passed to restrict the amount of trees that could be felled. The ironmasters were also competing with the demands for timber by the Royal Navy, which took precedence, and so they began to look further afield for suitable sites to set up smelting works.

One of these Sussex ironmasters, Anthony Morley, established a small works at Pontygwaith on the banks of the river Taff, six miles south of the village of Merthyr, in 1583. Ironstone was probably easy to come by, being found as nodules in the river, and the valley of the Taff was well forested. Very little is known about the operation of this works. It may have cast cannon and cannonballs for the Royal Navy, but it was most likely concerned principally with producing pig iron which was shipped elsewhere for refining. Morley eventually lost control of the Pontygwaith furnace in a bankruptcy suit, but by 1640 it was still in production, under the ownership of Messrs Lewis and Cook, the latter being another Sussex ironmaster. At about the same time another small blast furnace was erected at Blaencanaid, on the hillside immediately south of Merthyr, traces of which can still be seen today. It is not known when either of these works ceased production, or why. Operations may well have been seasonal as there would have been insufficient water to drive a wheel during the dry seasons, and output was small. Certainly the isolated location of Merthyr, and the difficulties of transporting the finished product, were factors in their decline.

The introduction of the coke fired furnace resulted in the iron industry being located in coalfield areas. The first coke fired furnace in South Wales was set up at Hirwaun in 1757, followed by the opening of the Dowlais works in 1759. Here the blast furnace was erected by a partnership led by Isaac Wilkinson, an ironmaster from Bersham in Clwyd. Situated on the hillside above Merthyr it was not ideally located, but Wilkinson and his partners had secured an extensive mineral lease, for an annual ground rent of a mere £31, allowing them to obtain their raw materials very cheaply. Partnered by John Guest, an ironmaster from Broseley in Shropshire, Wilkinson built another blast furnace in 1763 on the banks of the Taff, on land leased from the Earl of Plymouth. However lack of progress here prompted them to sell their interest in it, and in 1765 the new Plymouth works became the property of Anthony Bacon.

Anthony Bacon, a native of Cumberland, had arrived in Merthyr in 1763. In 1765 he not only became the owner of the Plymouth works, but also, with his partner William Brownrigg, established the Cyfarthfa works on the banks of the Taff. Cyfarthfa was the best located of the Merthyr ironworks, with a plentiful water supply and a mineral lease extending over 4,000 acres at an annual rent of £100. For the next 60 years production at Cyfarthfa was to outstrip those of its neighbours.

These three works had one furnace each and concentrated on producing pig iron. The American War of Independence between 1776 and 1783 provided lucrative contracts for the Merthyr ironmasters from the Royal Navy. Consequently foundries were established to cast cannon and cannonballs. One of them was built on the site of the later Ynysfach works, and in 1782 was leased to Francis Homfray who cast cannon with pig iron from the Cyfarthfa furnace. However Homfray soon departed, to be succeeded by Richard Crawshay from Normanton in Yorkshire. When Anthony Bacon retired in 1783 Crawshay gained control of the Cyfarthfa works, while the Plymouth works was taken over by Richard Hill. Homfray, meanwhile, was busy establishing a new ironworks at Penydarren, which opened in 1784.

The biggest problem faced by the ironmasters was the transportation of iron from Merthyr to the small port at Cardiff. The route they inherited was based on the old Roman road between Merthyr Tydfil and Caerphilly which involved negotiating steep hills and was wholly unsuitable. Under the Glamorganshire Turnpike Act of 1771, instigated by Anthony Bacon, a new road was constructed along the Taff valley to Tongwynlais, four miles north of Cardiff.

The Pontygwaith ironworks, painted by an unknown artist in the seventeenth century.

Whereas Isaac Wilkinson and Anthony Bacon were the real founders of Merthyr's iron industry, by the 1780s the name of Richard Crawshay began to dominate events. The Guests were to achieve their reputation later, while the Homfray and Hill families played secondary roles throughout. Crawshay was quick to see that the main market lay in producing bar and not pig iron, and immediately took out a licence to use Cort's puddling process when it was patented in 1784. At Dowlais the lack of success in applying Peter Onions' process dissuaded all but Guest from investing in puddling. The Penydarren works began to produce bar iron in 1788, buying in pig iron from Dowlais. Similarly Cyfarthfa bought in pig iron from Dowlais and Plymouth for refining.

Production was now increasing rapidly—at Cyfarthfa production of bar iron rose from 2,300 tons in 1790 to 6,000 tons in 1798. The turnpike road of 1771 was already hopelessly inadequate, but with thriving businesses and a ready market for their products the Merthyr ironmasters were able to raise the capital necessary to construct a canal from Merthyr to Cardiff. The Glamorganshire Canal Act was passed by Parliament in 1790. All four ironmasters were shareholders in

Richard Crawshay (1739-1810).

the new company, but Richard Crawshay held by far the largest share. Within four years the canal had been completed, and the head of the canal had been extended back to the Cyfarthfa works, to the obvious advantage of Crawshay. Disagreements with Crawshay over the tariffs to be charged on the canal encouraged the other three ironmasters to construct a tramroad from Penydarren to the canal at Abercynon in 1802. Although output of iron was to rise dramatically, causing congestion and delays on the canal, it was the canal itself that provided the stimulus without which demand could not have been met.

In 1784 Merthyr Tydfil had four blast furnaces. By 1812 this figure had risen to 18, which could produce up to 850 tons of pig iron per week. Steam blowing engines, which replaced waterwheel powered bellows, were installed first at Dowlais in 1798, to be followed at the Ynysfach works, opened by Crawshay as an extension of the Cyfarthfa works in 1801. At Penydarren Samuel Homfray had employed Richard Trevithick to experiment with high pressure steam engines, but Trevithick's association with Merthyr is remembered now for one momentous event—on 21 February 1804 one of Trevithick's locomotives completed a ten mile journey from Merthyr to Abercynon on the Penydarren Tramroad, and thus became the first steam locomotive ever to run on rails.

The Revolutionary and Napoleonic Wars with France between 1793 and 1815 had created an unprecedented demand for both wrought and cast iron products. However this would eventually appear less significant compared to post war expansion. The total of 18 blast furnaces in 1812 had risen to 41 when the iron industry in Merthyr reached its zenith in about 1850. This figure includes the four new blast furnaces erected at the Ifor works, which opened as an extension to Dowlais in 1839. The sight of this activity presented an awesome spectacle to visitors, as Charles Cliffe noted when he visted Merthyr in 1848: 'The scene is strange and impressive in broad daylight, but when viewed at night is wild beyond conception .... The vivid glow and roaring of the blast furnaces near at hand—the lurid light of distant works—the clanking of hammers and rolling mills, the confused din of massive machinery—the burning headlands—the coke hearths, now if the night be stormy, bursting into sheets of flame, now rapt in vast and impenetrable clouds of smoke—the wild figures of the workmen, the actors in this apparently infernal scene—all combined to impress the mind of the spectator wonderfully.'

By the end of the Napoleonic Wars there had also been changes in the management of the works. At Dowlais John Guest had been succeeded by his son Thomas in 1787, to be followed again by his son, Josiah John Guest, in 1807. It was largely his vision and business acumen that enabled Dowlais to achieve its status of the largest works in the world. A liberal who advocated free

The head of the Glamorganshire Canal at Cyfarthfa, drawn by William Pamplin in about 1800. Next to it is Cyfarthfa House, built by Anthony Bacon, which remained the Crawshays' home until 1810.

trade, and who was elected Merthyr's first MP after the 1832 Reform Act, he was responsible for providing the first educational facilities for workers in Merthyr—at Dowlais Stables in 1828—and served on the first Merthyr Board of Health. Nevertheless he was resolutely opposed to Chartism and trade unions. At the Plymouth Works Richard Hill died in 1806, to be succeeded by his sons Anthony and Richard. Anthony remained in charge of the works until his own death in 1862. Richard Crawshay died in 1810 and his son William Crawshay I directed operations from his office in Bell Yard, London. The day to day management of the works was left to William Crawshay II who presided over the great expansion at Cyfarthfa, and who also inadvisedly spent £30,000 of the company's capital resources to build Cyfarthfa Castle in 1825, his vast picturesque mansion overlooking the works. Opinions differ as to its architectural merit but it certainly exudes all the swagger of the successful industrialist. The Homfray family sold their interest in Penydarren in 1822 on the death of Samuel Homfray. Thereafter the works continued under the partnership of Thompson and Foreman.

In 1821 the rails for the Stockton and Darlington Railway were produced at the Dowlais works. Penydarren also engaged in producing rails at an early date, supplying the Liverpool and Manchester Railway, but it was Cyfarthfa and Dowlais that reaped the rewards of the railway boom of the 1830s and 1840s. At Dowlais the Big Mill was constructed to produce rails in 1830, to be supplemented by the Little Mill in 1840, while at Cyfarthfa a new mill was built in 1833. The list of foreign orders received at Dowlais is impressive—Baltimore and Susquihanna Railway (1835), Berlin and

The Ynysfach ironworks in about 1815, painted by Penry Williams, with the Glamorganshire Canal in the foreground. The engine house depicted was replaced in about 1836 by the engine house which still stands today.

Leipzig Railway (1836), St Petersburg-Pauloffsky Railway (1836) and the New Orleans and Nashville Railway (1836). Both Dowlais and Cyfarthfa supplied rails to the East India Co and had considerable success at home as well, even in the Midlands where there was fierce competition from the Black Country ironworks. During the 1840s Cyfarthfa supplied the Midland, York and North Midland, Preston & Wyr, and Eastern Counties Railways, while Dowlais received contracts from the Great Western, South Eastern and the Dover and East Counties Railways.

The boom in demand for iron bar and rails inevitably led to overproduction. The iron industry experienced several periods of recession when the price of iron fell and surpluses were created. There were a number of attempts to negotiate an agreement amongst iron-

Sir Josiah John Guest (1787-1852).

William Crawshay II (1788-1867).

masters to reduce the amount of iron produced, thereby pushing up prices, but they met with little success in South Wales. Dowlais was better able to withstand these fluctuations in the market, partly because their business was more profitable, but also because they were careful to invest in any new technology that would decrease production costs. Even as early as 1832 William Crawshay III wrote to his father saying that 'new and more up to date engineers' were needed at Cyfarthfa because their 'iron is inferior to Dowlais and certainly not the best made.' At Dowlais they had adopted the hot blast technique, i.e. blowing hot rather than cold air into the blast furnaces, which had been patented in 1828 and which substantially reduced the amount of coke required for smelting. Cyfarthfa and Penydarren were slow to follow suit, but it was the Plymouth works that really lagged behind. There water power continued in use long after it became obsolescent, and in order to re-use the water supply the works had to expand into three separate plants—the Pentre-

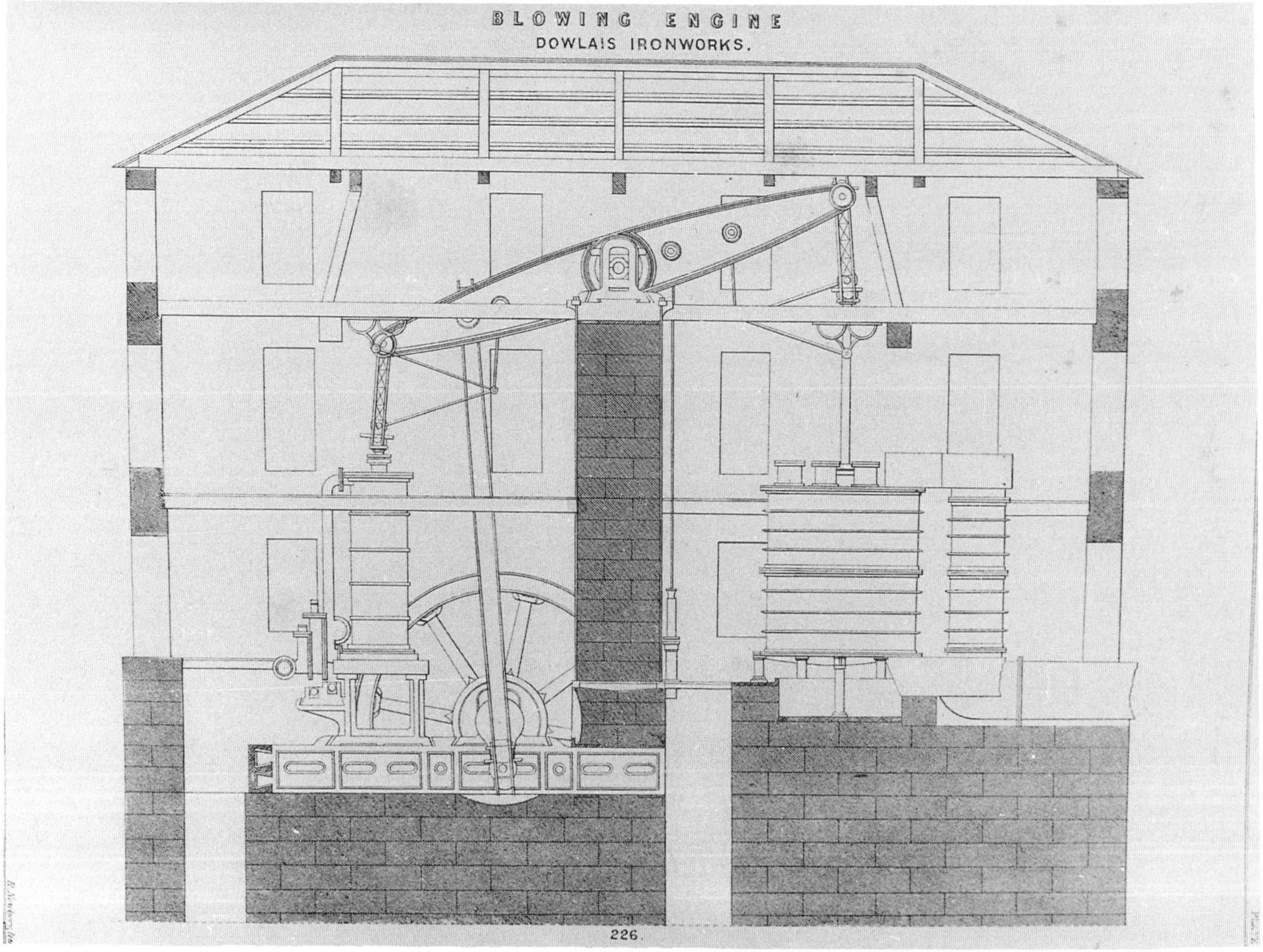

To improve the efficiency of the blast furnaces steam engines were employed to work the blowing cylinders. This engine was in use at Dowlais in the 1860s.

bach Forge and Dyffryn Furnaces being added—stretched over a distance of nearly three miles. After the dry summers of 1843 and 1844 steam power was finally introduced and output rose dramatically from nearly 13,000 tons in 1840 to over 35,000 tons in 1846, the same year that Dowlais produced 85,000 tons of iron.

However the Dowlais Iron Co was not without its problems either. The leasehold covering the works and mineral rights was due to expire in 1848, and negotiations with the landowner John, the Second Marquis of Bute, began as early as 1841. The Marquis of Bute felt that in drawing up new terms he should receive

A method of ironstone mining known as patching, which was particularly favoured at Dowlais, and which destroyed the agricultural potential of the land.

Working Iron at Merthyr Tydfil, a watercolour by J. C. Ibbetson, painted in 1792, showing the puddled mass of iron being hammered to remove slag.

The Penydarren Works in 1817, painted by Thomas Hornor—'the inhabitants proudly ask the stranger if he has viewed it [Merthyr] from the surrounding heights after nightfall? Should he answer in the negative, they tell him he has not seen Merthyr'.

compensation for the over generous terms of the original lease. Although he had a valid argument the proposals he drew up were ridiculous and unworkable. They included a fine of £80,000 for renewing the lease, an annual rent of £9,000 (compared to the previous £31), plus royalties on all iron produced. Further negotiations got nowhere, and in November 1847 the Guests were resigned to leaving Dowlais. By February 1848 three of the blast furnaces had been blown out and machinery had been brought up from the mines ready for sale. Then 44 days before the lease expired, the Marquis of Bute died unexpectedly. Negotiations were now the responsibility of the Bute Trustees and new, more favourable, terms were quickly agreed. The formal agreement was not signed until 1853, just two months after the death of Sir Josiah John Guest.

Living and Working in Merthyr

In 1845 over 18,000 people were employed in the ironworks of Merthyr Tydfil, out of a total population of about 40,000. While the achievements of the Guests and the Crawshays have been written about on many occasions much less attention has been paid to the people who actually produced the iron. During the 1840s, when Merthyr's iron industry was at its peak, there was a focus of attention on the working conditions and standard of living of the people of Merthyr Tydfil. This started with enquiries made by the Children's Employment Commission who published their report in 1842. In 1850 a report into the sanitary condition of Merthyr Tydfil, which includes much information on working people, was made under the auspices of the General Board of Health. Between 1849 and 1851 the *Morning Chronicle* published a series of detailed articles from its correspondents, who were sent to report on life and work in Britain's industrial districts. These are just three of the documents that give us a valuable insight into the lives of ordinary people engaged by the ironworks of Merthyr Tydfil.

In less than a century Merthyr had grown from a village with about 40 houses in a fairly prosperous agricultural area to a large industrial town—easily the largest in Wales. Its workforce was therefore made up almost entirely of recent immigrants. In the early years of the industry only a small workforce was required. Technological expertise was imported from other ironworking districts like Shropshire and the Midlands—Charles Wood, for example, who built the first furnace at Cyfarthfa, came from Wolverhampton. It may be that skilled workers like furnacemen were also drawn from these areas, attracted to Wales by the prospect of good wages and decent houses.

However the rapid expansion of the industry brought with it a demand for a large skilled and unskilled workforce in what was a very labour intensive industry. Employment in the iron industry, for all its hardships, was nonetheless work, and offered much better rates of pay than agricultural labouring. Many people, no longer able to work on the land, had no option but to travel to places like Merthyr in search of a living. Merthyr's workforce came mainly from rural Glamorgan and the depressed agricultural districts of west and mid Wales. When iron ore began to be imported this attracted immigrants from other areas such as Cumberland and Somerset, and Merthyr also had a sizeable Irish, and later Jewish community.

William Williams, Overman of the Cyfarthfa forges in 1842.

It is very difficult to obtain accurate statistics of the number of people employed at any one time in the

South Tunnel Pit, one of the Dowlais Iron Co collieries, showing its water balance headgear, the means by which coal was brought to the surface in most Merthyr collieries.

works. When William Williams, overman of the Cyfarthfa works, was questioned about this in 1842 he could only reply that in the forges and rolling mills 'there are, as near as I am able to say, upwards of 2,000 people employed; as men work in gangs on job-work by the piece they employ whom they choose, consequently no real account of numbers can be given.' While men were employed for the most skilled and heavy labour, many women and children were employed on 'light' work because they could be paid at a lower rate. Children were brought to work not directly by the company, but by their parents. If a collier or puddler employed his boy to assist him he could receive extra pay, which economic circumstances forced most of them to do. Officially the companies all disapproved of this, but in practice, with the exception of Anthony Hill who in 1849 tried but failed to ban children under ten from working underground, they did nothing to prevent it. Similarly women and young girls could get work by joining the teams of limestone breakers and tip girls which were organised on a basis similar to which vegetable picking is still carried out today.

Work in the collieries and ironstone mines was based on 10-12 hour shifts, and most people worked seven days a week. During the winter months many of them never saw daylight for weeks. Although Sir Humphry Davy's safety lamp had been invented years previously they were not widely used in the collieries at Merthyr even as late as the 1860s. In 1842 Benjamin Martin, mineral agent at Penydarren, told the Children's

Employment Commission: 'The miners have Davy lamps to go into the workings in the morning to see that the air is pure, but they never work by them—they are never allowed to work in places where the air requires them to use Davy lamps.' To lessen the danger of explosion of gases, known as fire-damp, collieries were constructed with furnace shafts. These had a fire burning at the base of them and ensured a constant flow of air underground.

Nevertheless the use of naked flames inevitably caused some underground explosions, the worst of which were at Cyfarthfa's Gethin collieries in 1862 and 1865, when there were 47 and 22 fatalities respectively. Air doors were fitted underground to contain any explosions, and these were operated by children as young as six years old. Robert Franks, one of the government inspectors who collected evidence for the Children's Employment Commission, wrote of Mary Davis, a seven year old air door keeper at one of the Plymouth collieries: 'A very pretty little girl, who was fast asleep under a piece of rock near the air door below ground. Her lamp had gone out for want of oil; and, upon waking her, she said the rats had run away with her bread and cheese, so she went to sleep.' No doubt her tiredness was induced by excessive labour in what must have been a very lonely occupation for a girl of seven.

The other task for which children were employed underground was in loading and pulling trams, known locally as *drams*. Although horses were used underground, in many of the levels the roofs were too low for them, so children, from the age of about 11 upwards, had to take their place. Henrietta Frankland, in 1842 an 11 year old drammer, gives a graphic description of what the job entailed: 'When well I draw the drams, which contain 4 to 5 cwt of coal, from the head to the main road; I make 48 to 50 journeys [per 12 hour shift]. The mine is wet where we work, as the water passes through the roof, and the workings are only 30 to 33 inches high."

Employment was hardly any less strenuous at the works itself, particularly on the blast furnaces. Once brought to the works the coal was converted to coke. In the early years this was done by smouldering it in open heaps, but later special ovens were constructed for the purpose. Similarly the ironstone had to be roasted in

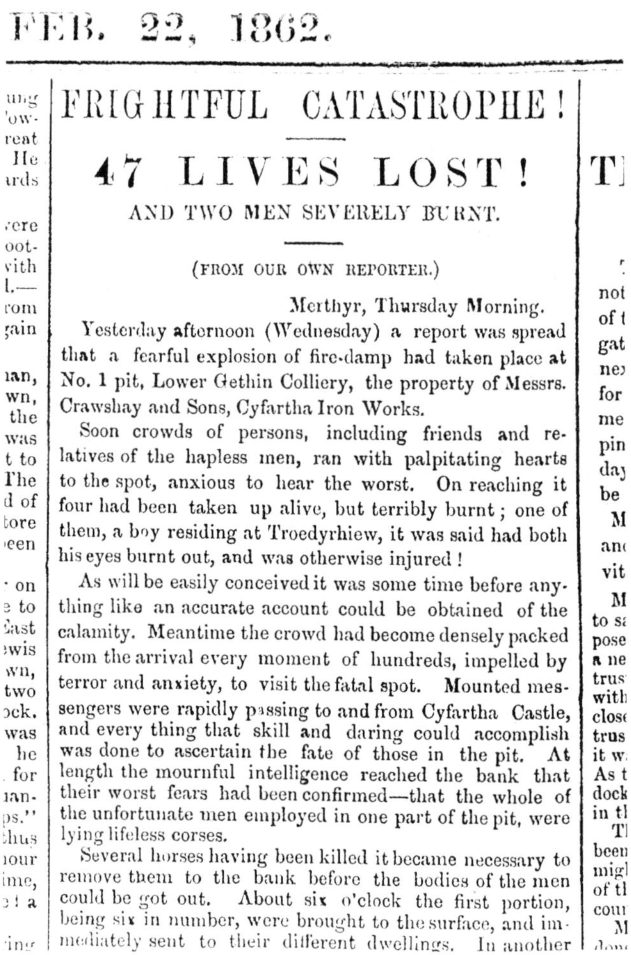

FEB. 22, 1862.

FRIGHTFUL CATASTROPHE!

47 LIVES LOST!

AND TWO MEN SEVERELY BURNT.

(FROM OUR OWN REPORTER.)

Merthyr, Thursday Morning.

Yesterday afternoon (Wednesday) a report was spread that a fearful explosion of fire-damp had taken place at No. 1 pit, Lower Gethin Colliery, the property of Messrs. Crawshay and Sons, Cyfartha Iron Works.

Soon crowds of persons, including friends and relatives of the hapless men, ran with palpitating hearts to the spot, anxious to hear the worst. On reaching it four had been taken up alive, but terribly burnt; one of them, a boy residing at Troedyrhiew, it was said had both his eyes burnt out, and was otherwise injured!

As will be easily conceived it was some time before anything like an accurate account could be obtained of the calamity. Meantime the crowd had become densely packed from the arrival every moment of hundreds, impelled by terror and anxiety, to visit the fatal spot. Mounted messengers were rapidly passing to and from Cyfartha Castle, and every thing that skill and daring could accomplish was done to ascertain the fate of those in the pit. At length the mournful intelligence reached the bank that their worst fears had been confirmed—that the whole of the unfortunate men employed in one part of the pit, were lying lifeless corses.

Several horses having been killed it became necessary to remove them to the bank before the bodies of the men could be got out. About six o'clock the first portion, being six in number, were brought to the surface, and immediately sent to their different dwellings. In another

Accidents in the works and collieries were frequent, often resulting in death or disablement, but only a few of them made the headlines.

special calcining kilns before it was ready for smelting. Both these operations required a large number of labourers to unload the drams and load the kilns and ovens. The limestone was used untreated, but the stone from the quarries had to be broken up, for which women were employed. At Dowlais in 1842 Hannah Jenkins, aged 21, and her helper Elizabeth Davis, aged 16, were required to break enough limestone to supply one furnace—about 12 tons over a 12 hour shift.

An artist's impression of a drammer working underground which originally appeared in the report of the Children's Employment Commission.

Filling the blast furnaces was one of the most dangerous and generally unhealthy jobs in the industry—'many of the young people drop off from 18 to 22 years of age, of a species of consumption' as John Jones, overman of the Cyfarthfa furnaces, so delicately put it. The furnaces were kept in blast continually not only to maximise production, but because if they were allowed to cool the firebrick casing would crack and the furnace would have to be shut down and relined. At Dowlais, however, they did manage to adopt the custom of stopping the blowing engines for about ten hours on a Sunday, although this was partly to facilitate maintenance and the furnaces were not allowed to cool excessively. The furnaces therefore required constant charging. This was done by loading the raw materials into a barrow, the contents of which were tipped manually into the top of the furnace.

Tapping the molten iron was the job of the furnaceman, and was the most skilled job on the furnaces. He had to be able to judge the quality of the iron as it flowed out of the furnace—'When the stream of molten metal runs too thin, he says, "She scours, we must give her more mine". If, on the other hand, the metal flows curdy and thick, he says, "She gobs, and must have more lime" '. Experienced furnacemen performed this task with casual effortless, as was noted by one onlooker in 1868: 'you see the molten metal [actually slag] running out of a spout into an iron truck .... A man goes up to the wheeled cauldron, dips his spade into it like a spoon into a jar of treacle, and examines what he brings out just as if he was going to taste it. Another man wants to light his pipe, and so he dips a rod into the molten metal, and applies the glowing button he fishes up to his pipe bowl as ordinary smokers use a commonplace Vesuvian.'

The molten iron was run out on to the floor of the casting shed and into sand beds made up by the moulders. An idea of the amount of labour required to operate the furnaces is given by Hugh Morgan, master of the six furnaces at Penydarren. On Sundays the

Tip girls at the Dowlais works. Their job was to help clear the drams of the burning cinders from the blast furnaces, work carried out in all weathers.

remainder of the works was closed, with only the minimum labour force required to keep the furnaces in blast. 'The limestone girls do not work on Sundays, or those emptying coal; the persons we have employed on Sundays are six furnace-keepers, six fillers, six cinder-fillers, six girls filling coals, three or four helpers, four boys at the hot blast stoves, and three at the engines.' The entire labour force employed on the smelting of iron, including the calcining and coking, was much higher. At Dowlais in 1842 over 1,000 people worked on the 18 blast furnaces.

Relief for the poor in Merthyr was wholly inadequate. Until the Union Workhouse, pictured here, opened in 1853 only some of the homeless or orphaned children found shelter, usually among the poverty stricken Irish community.

Even greater numbers were employed in the forges and rolling mills. After the pig iron had been remelted in a refining furnace and formed into cakes, or 'pig moulds', it was broken up using two-handled sledge hammers operated by two men, ready for puddling. Contemporary paintings and engravings that show the refining processes always show some of the workers busily engaged in their work, while others are just hanging around seeming to do nothing. The nature of the work here meant that much of it involved intermittent bursts of activity followed by periods of waiting, unlike the blast furnaces where the labour was constant.

The puddlers were among the most highly paid and highly skilled of workers, and they worked in eight rather than 12 hour shifts. Stirring the semi-molten, white-hot mass of iron exposed these men to intense

Cyfarthfa at night, painted by Penry Williams in 1825, showing the puddling furnaces and rolling mills.

heat and the brightness of the furnace hearth damaged their eyes. Puddling was a slow process during which time the iron changed in consistency from a frothy fluid-like appearance, which by stirring with a long bar changed to 'a crumbling fineness like snow powder' before it began to clot into an amorphous, semi-molten mass of iron. At this point the puddler lifted the iron out with a pair of long handled tongs, and placed it on a truck which his underhand, usually a boy, had ready.

The boy then rushed the mass of iron to the forge hammers where the slag was beaten out and the iron was shaped into a bar ready for rolling. This was described by the correspondent of the *Morning Chronicle* thus: 'the rough bar is next snatched by huge pincers and swung with a vigorous arm upon iron rollers, of great strength and thickness, and in rapid motion,

The blast furnaces at Dowlais, painted by G. Childs in 1840.

through which it passes—being grasped on the other side by a man handling a huge tongs, suspended by a chain to the roof, who returns it over the rollers to the workman on the other side, who next puts it through a second and smaller groove in the rollers—and so on till the bar is lengthened to the proper extent, and reduced to the required width. In the course of this operation any dross which the 'squeezers' failed to eliminate is squeezed out by the rollers. The bar is generally 12ft long and 3in wide, and whilst red hot and flexible as a thong of leather, it is dragged out by boys and sometimes by girls. The whole of this process takes less time than it has occupied the reader to peruse this account of it.'

The above is only a brief description of some of the jobs in the ironworks. For every stage in the manufacturing process there were skilled workers and an army of helpers to assist them. Also industrial enterprises of this size required large maintenance staff such as engineers, blacksmiths, carpenters and masons. Firebricks to line the furnaces were produced at each works, as was the lime used to cement them together.

Merthyr Tydfil High Street in 1850. 'The roadways of the streets . . . are in rainy weather . . . a mass of festering black mud, into which the wheels of the carts which carry coal to the houses sink deeply.'.

Rates of pay were never constant, fluctuating according to the price that iron fetched on the market. Some employees were paid a fixed wage, others were paid on a piece work basis by the job or the ton. Rates of pay were broadly similar at each of the works, but the ironmasters never attempted to formulate a common wages policy. In 1842 limestone breakers could earn up to 8 shillings for a 72 hour week, with 5 shillings for their helpers. Helpers to fill the blast furnaces earned 3s 6d a week, helpers at straightening bar about 6d per day. John Jenkins, a 16 year old shearer at the Dowlais Old Forge, told the Children's Employment Commission; 'My wages are now 9s per week; they were 11s before "the fall" a short time back'.

Skilled workers commanded much higher wages. Men like puddlers and rollermen were difficult to replace and the companies had to pay sufficient for them not to be tempted to take their expertise elsewhere. In 1840 puddlers at the Cyfarthfa Works earned £6 per month, but by 1849 this figure had fallen to £3/16. The comparative figures for colliers was £4/10 and £3, rollermen producing bar £21 and £12, and furnacemen £5/9 and £4/11.

These skilled workers also received preferential treatment with regard to housing, which until well after the mid nineteenth century was almost always provided by the company, to whom tenants paid a fixed rent.

The Triangle at Pentrebach, begun in about 1839.

Cyfarthfa operated a policy of giving skilled workers four-roomed houses, and unskilled workers two-roomed houses. Single unskilled workers were often less fortunate since no housing was provided for them at all. However lodgings were easy to come by, ranging from the dingy cellar dwellings of Merthyr's Chinatown, where the Irish community lived, to sharing a room in the house of a skilled worker.

One of the rows of houses built for skilled workers at Cyfarthfa was Chapel Row. These were large four-roomed houses built in about 1825. In 1851 no 4 Chapel Row was home for 12 people, which included Daniel Parry, the head of the house who had been a puddler at the Cyfarthfa works since the 1820s, who lived there with his wife and five children. The other five members of the household were lodgers who must have shared a single room. Because the workforce were employed in shifts this often meant that two or more people shared the same bed. This sub-letting of accommodation was an opportunity to improve their income which skilled workers readily took advantage of.

The rapid growth of the town in the first half of the nineteenth century, and the absence of any public body to regulate it, created urban squalor and severe public

David Square, Abercanaid, built in about 1850.

health problems, a situation usually blamed on shabby housing. Although the houses were often too small for the families that lived in them, they were nonetheless very well built—sandstone for building was easily available as it was a by-product of iron mining, and coal was available cheaply so the rooms could all have fireplaces. The furnishing of the houses varied enormously. One observer noted at Cyfarthfa Row, built for skilled workers in 1840: 'In the kitchen were two mahogany chests of drawers, each of which supported a looking glass .... There was also a well-polished eight-day clock, and a set of good mahogany chairs'. Others were not so fortunate: 'In the first house we entered, inhabited by an Irishman, there sat hovering over the fire a man swollen with dropsy; the house had no other furniture than a three-legged table, a small bench, two stools and a few utensils for cooking, such as saucepans, basins, plates and crockery. Upstairs were three beds of hay, without a single article of furniture'. Houses were kept spotlessly clean, in marked contrast to what lay beyond the front door.

The problem lay in the fact that houses were built in closely packed rows, and that the supply of fresh water and sanitary facilities were woefully inadequate. The river Taff was an open sewer, further contaminated with dead dogs and offal from slaughter houses. The overflowing privies were mostly unusable, people having to make do with the tips and river banks, and the stench in summer must have been unbearable. Disease was prone to spread rapidly, and there were several outbreaks of cholera and typhoid. The cholera epidemic of 1849 claimed 1,400 lives in five months, and many families had to be evacuated from their homes to halt the spread of the disease. The study of the sanitary condition and water supply, and its effects on the inhabitants of the town, produced by the General Board of Health in 1850, documented the worst conditions in minute detail. Much of it makes gruesome reading that reflects shame on the people with authority in the town.

On the brighter side there were some more enlightened approaches to urban planning adopted by the Plymouth works. Because the works had been set up on three different sites its housing stock could be built as a series of small villages. The supply of water was better than elsewhere and the shared privies were not overused. These villages suffered much less from cholera epidemics than other parts of Merthyr. Among their notable achievements was the Triangle at Pentrebach which was a novel arrangement of three rows of houses facing each other, and an exemplary piece of community architecture. Better still were three parallel rows of houses known as the Squares, which were built alongside the Glamorganshire Canal at Abercanaid in a rural setting. Alas both the Squares and Triangle have now been demolished.

The social life of the workforce was naturally limited by excessive hours of work. Religious and cultural life was centred on the chapel, most of which were Welsh

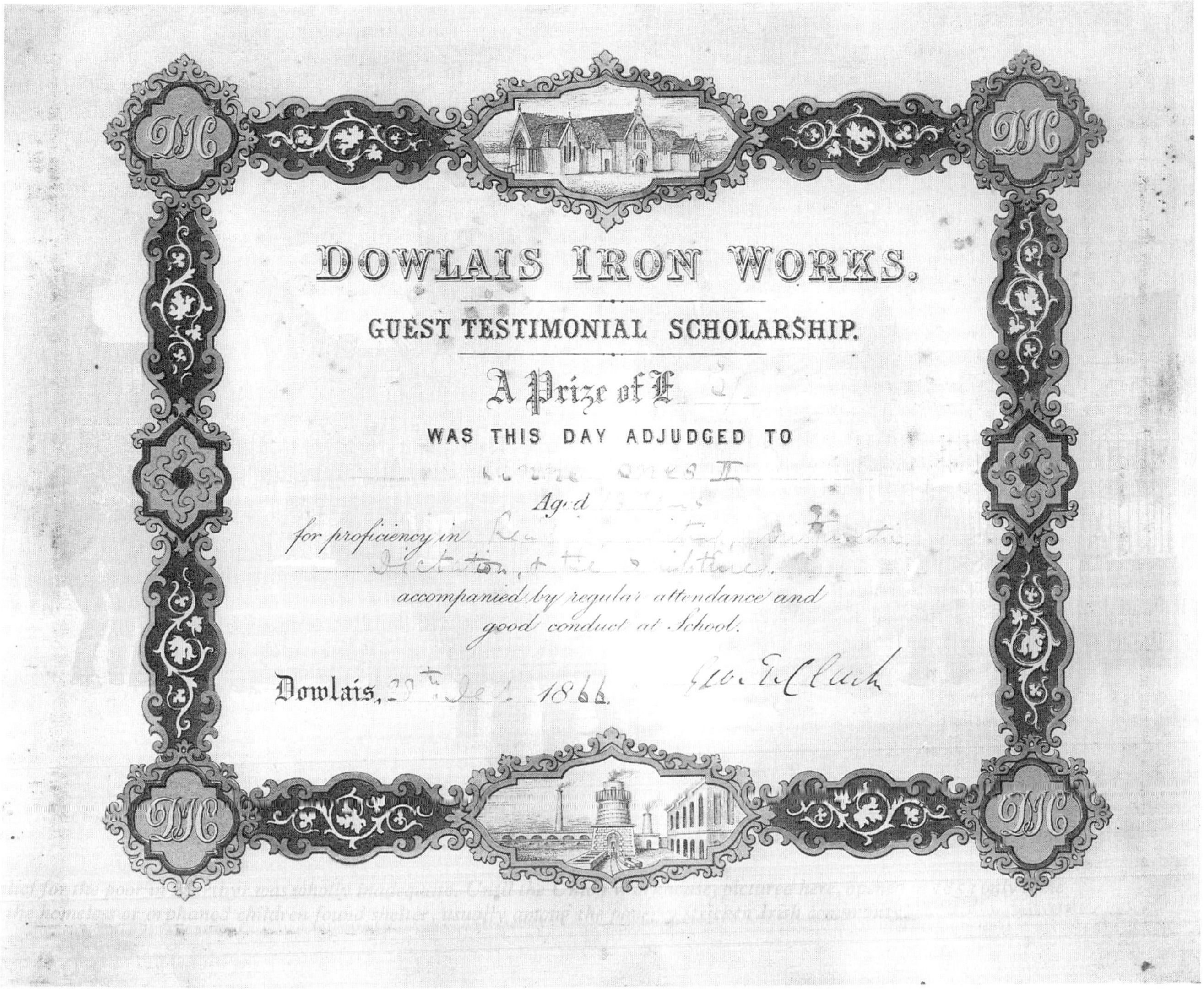
DOWLAIS IRON WORKS.

GUEST TESTIMONIAL SCHOLARSHIP.

A Prize of £

WAS THIS DAY ADJUDGED TO

Aged

for proficiency in

accompanied by regular attendance and good conduct at School.

Dowlais, 29th Oct 1866.

A certificate issued to a pupil of the Dowlais works school in 1866.

speaking. According to Anthony Hill, 'The Welsh people will not be driven, and they are strongly attached to their language .... The efforts being made to promote the greater spread of the native Welsh language is a great bar to the improvement of the people'. Nevertheless the efforts made by the English ironmasters to promote the Anglican church met with little success. The chapel was at the centre of a thriving musical tradition, although the Cyfarthfa Works had its own brass band, and most children received some education at the Sunday Schools. The Dowlais works opened its first school in 1828 in a room in Dowlais Stables. In

A typical pub scene—a good time was no doubt had by all. Men who had been disabled from accidents in the works often took up harp playing and eked out a precarious living playing in pubs.

1852 this was replaced by a newly built school, for which the company went to the expense of commissioning Sir Charles Barry, architect of the Houses of Parliament, to design.

The image of a chapel going, temperance minded community is, however, a touch misleading. 'Marriages are much too early about this quarter, from the intercourse of the sexes and nature of employment'. This was a polite way of saying that in Merthyr children lost their innocence early. 'The public houses are more the resort of young persons than the Sunday-schools or chapels', William Williams, overman at Cyfarthfa, complained in 1842. The sweltering heat of an ironworks, and the shortage of fresh water, gave the workforce an appetite for vast quantities of beer. At Cyfarthfa the wages were paid out in the company's own public houses, which doubtless encouraged some to drink to excess. Merthyr must have had some of the liveliest pubs in Wales, and it was in some of these, like the Three Horseshoes in Georgetown, that the seeds of Merthyr's radical politics were sown.

Competition and Decline

The second half of the nineteenth century was one of increasing competition and decline for the Merthyr ironworks. Ironmaking was never again to be as profitable as it had been during the railway boom of the 1830s and 1840s, and their decline was to be almost as swift as their rise to prominence.

One of the many difficulties that beset the ironmasters was the supply of raw materials. Coal was no problem, but the local ironstone had a low iron content and had to be roasted in a calcining kiln before it could be smelted, which increased the cost of production. Also, as reserves became depleted it was necessary to work at greater depths to win the ore. As early as the 1820s the Plymouth works had leased iron ore mines at Bigrigg and Crowgarth in West Cumberland, and throughout the 1840s supplies of ore for Cyfarthfa and Dowlais were regularly shipped from Furness, West Cumberland, the Forest of Dean, and the Brendon Hills in Somerset. By 1856 over half of the pig iron made at Dowlais came from imported ore.

Given the importance of locating iron production close to the source of raw materials the new iron producing centres of Cleveland, the Cumbrian coast, and in Lincolnshire and Northamptonshire, were able to produce iron much more economically. These new works were often set up using Welsh expertise, just as in Wales technological assistance had come from Shropshire, and soon South Wales was to fall behind in the technological race. Furthermore, in the main export markets of France, Germany and America, which Cyfarthfa and Dowlais had exploited so effectively, domestic production had been increased, again making use of British technology, leaving a shrinking export market.

In the fiercely competitive market of the 1850s it was inevitable that the smaller, older works would suffer. In 1859 Messrs Fothergill and Hankey, who had gained control of the Penydarren works after the death of William Thompson in 1854, decided to cease production altogether. A further indication of the increasing difficulties faced by the Merthyr ironmasters is that they began to mine coal for export. At Cyfarthfa, Castle Pit was opened in 1865 specifically for this purpose. The sale of the Penydarren works to Dowlais at a cost of nearly £60,000 included vast mineral deposits which the Dowlais Iron Co worked for the sale market. As William Jenkins, the Dowlais book keeper, noted in 1861, 'soon after the purchase of Penydarren, we commenced selling coal on a large scale. After June 1859 we made several large contracts for coal sent to Cardiff, Swansea, Liverpool, London, Hereford, Shrewsbury & c."

When the Cyfarthfa lease expired in 1864, Robert Thompson Crawshay could see no future for the iron industry in Merthyr, and it was only with great reluctance that he negotiated its renewal. Despite this pessimism, and the declining proportion of the nation's iron that South Wales produced, the industry still enjoyed periods of high demand and prosperity. The year of peak production in South Wales actually occurred in 1871 when there was a general boom in the economy. But alternated with periods of depression prospects were still gloomy. Wages were still based on the market price for iron, and reductions in pay were one thing that the workforce was not prepared to accept without a struggle. This, and reluctance of the ironmasters to recognise trade unions (Robert Thompson Crawshay would have nothing to do with them at all), were the cause of numerous strikes. The most serious of these began in April 1874 when a 10-20 per cent reduction in wages was announced. The ironmasters responded by imposing a lock-out at the works, and the strike ended in May 1875. However the Cyfarthfa furnaces remained shut down until the death of the intransigent Robert Thompson Crawshay in 1879.

In 1856 Henry Bessemer, at his experimental furnace in London, had developed a simpler process of producing what he termed 'malleable iron' than the puddling process that took two hours to convert 5cwt of pig into wrought iron. This malleable iron was in fact mild steel, which has a higher carbon content than wrought iron. True to its traditions the Dowlais works began experimenting with the new process, and after teething problems were overcome converted to producing limited quantities of steel in 1865. On the death of Sir Josiah John Guest in 1852 ownership of the works passed to his widow, Lady Charlotte, and in 1855 the management of the works passed into the hands of two trustees.

The Penydarren works in ruins, reputedly photographed by Robert Thompson Crawshay in the 1870s.

Castle Pit, which was opened in 1865 by the Cyfarthfa Iron Co to mine coal exclusively for the sale market.

A poster summing up the poor industrial relations that were a major characteristic of the 1870s.

Of these G. T. Clark, who had worked under Brunel on the Great Western Railway, was responsible for the manufacturing side of the business, and in 1856 he appointed William Menelaus as general manager of the works. Menelaus was the man behind the conversion to steel, and it was in large part due to him that Dowlais kept pace with technological developments and survived.

Plymouth and Cyfarthfa fared less well. When Anthony Hill died in 1862 the Plymouth works was sold for £250,000 to Messrs Fothergill, Hankey and Bateman. However working with obsolete technology and without the capital resources to convert to steel production, Plymouth closed in 1880, the company devoting itself purely to mining its vast reserves of coal. Cyfarthfa's conversion to steel began only after Robert Thompson Crawshay's death when his three sons, trading under the name of Crawshay Brothers (Cyfarthfa) Ltd, took control of the works. Four new iron clad furnaces were constructed and steel production started in 1884. At the Ynysfach works the four blast furnaces were relined and kept in reserve in case iron was needed again. However it is doubtful whether the furnaces were ever put back in blast.

For the production of steel the local ironstone was unsuitable because it had a high phosphorous content, and ironstone mining ceased altogether in Merthyr in the 1870s. Now that ore had to be imported, chiefly from Spain, production at Merthyr became a geographical anachronism. Recognising this the Dowlais Iron Co built an entirely new steelworks at East Moors in Cardiff in 1891. This began the final chapter of Merthyr's decline. In 1900 Dowlais was taken over by Arthur Keen of the Patent Nut and Bolt Co, and in 1902 the new company took over the Nettlefolds woodscrew manufacturing business to form GKN. At the same time it acquired the ailing Cyfarthfa works for an unspecified sum. Although some investment was made at Cyfarthfa it could not be worked profitably, and production ceased in 1910, with a brief reprieve during the First World War.

Investment at Dowlais proved more successful. In 1905 a new blast furnace complex was built which included two American designed 'Yankee' furnaces, and a new rail mill was added. Even so the attempt to construct a profitable modern steelworks on a site chosen to satisfy the demands of the eighteenth century, was really just the final prolonged period of decline. The Dowlais Works closed in 1930, too vulnerable to withstand a slump in the steel trade. All that survived into the post war period was a foundry on the site of the Ifor Works which was operated by the British Steel Corporation. This ceased production in 1987, ending over 200 years of Merthyr's association with the iron industry.

DOWLAIS MARKET-PLACE, CONVERTED TO THE RECEPTION OF PIT HORSES.

During the lock-out imposed by the ironmasters in 1874 all the pit ponies had to be brought up from the collieries.

Its heyday lasted little more than 100 years but it was a crucial period in British history which saw the transformation from an agrarian nation to an industrial one. It was a period of unprecedented progress in technology and material civilisation, but in the end the ironworks of Merthyr Tydfil, having contributed so much to this progress, became just another victim of it.

Had Merthyr not been able to diversify its economy to include coal mining the social consequences would have been catastrophic. Even so the legacy of the iron industry persisted into the twentieth century, principally in the form of poor housing, which by modern standards was socially unacceptable. From the mid nineteenth century onwards many people left Merthyr to emigrate to America, and in the 1930s many others left for south-east England. A government report produced at that time even suggested that Merthyr should be abandoned altogether. Undaunted by such nonsense

The Dowlais works after conversion to steel production.

The Cyfarthfa works after closure.

G. T. Clark (1809-1898).

William Menelaus (1818-1883).

much of the town has been rebuilt in the post war period, clearing away some of the gloomier reminders of its past.

The ironworks themselves went into rapid decay after closure, and traces of the Plymouth and Penydarren works have now all but vanished. At Cyfarthfa the seven blast furnaces, including four dating from the eighteenth century, have survived, as have the four at Ynysfach, two of which date from 1801. These are now Scheduled Ancient Monuments, receiving the same statutory protection as prehistoric monuments, and are unique and impressive remains. The surviving engine house at Ynysfach has recently been restored by the Merthyr Tydfil Heritage Trust, as has Dowlais Stables,

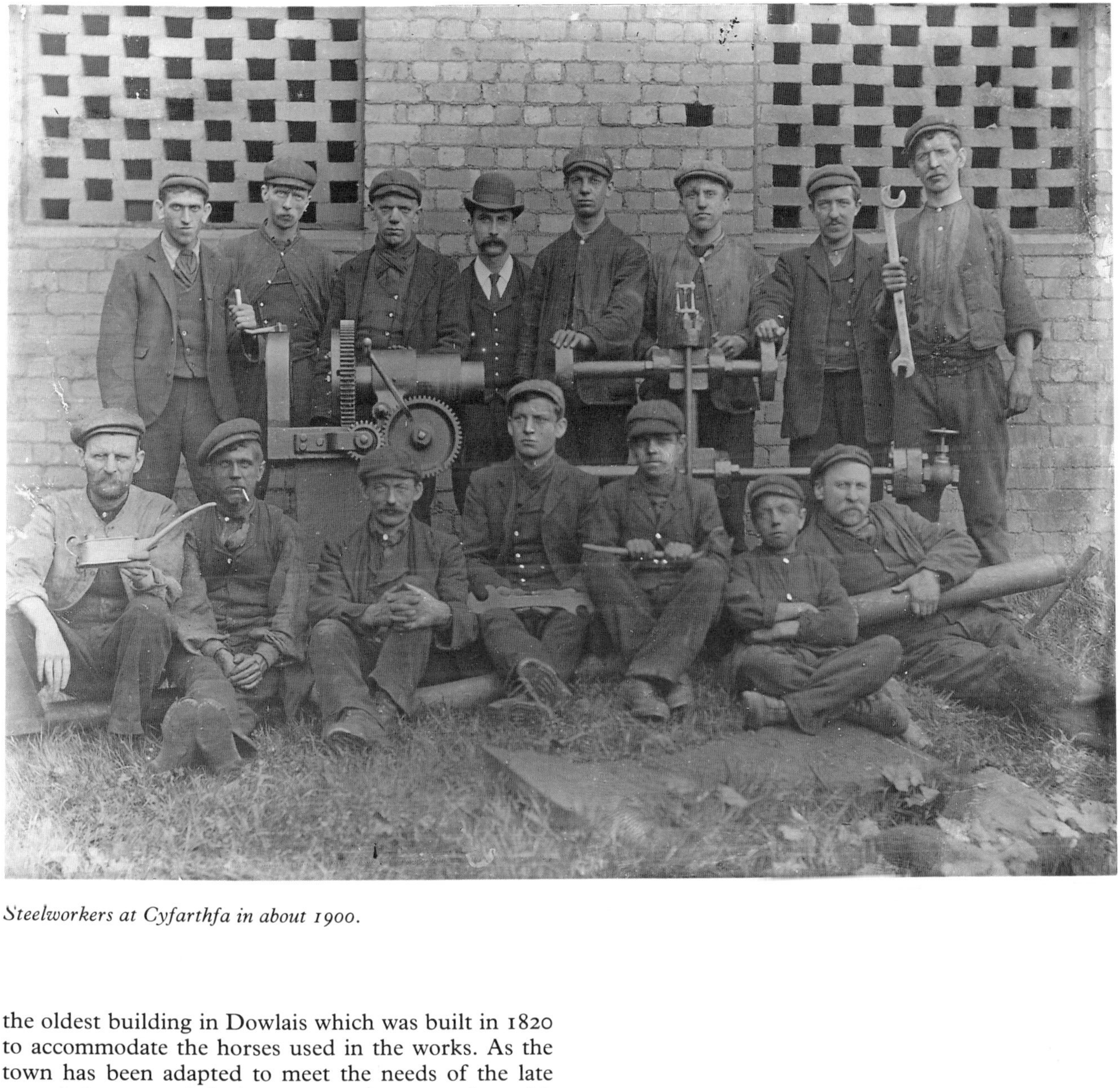

Steelworkers at Cyfarthfa in about 1900.

the oldest building in Dowlais which was built in 1820 to accommodate the horses used in the works. As the town has been adapted to meet the needs of the late twentieth century it is these restorations, together with the Cyfarthfa furnaces and Cyfarthfa Castle, that acknowledge Merthyr's proud place in British history.

Some Further Reading

Edgar Jones, *A History of GKN*, Vol I, 1759-1918, (1987).
J. B. Lowe, *Welsh Industrial Workers' Housing 1775-1875*, (1985).
J. P. Addis, *The Crawshay Dynasty*, (1957).
Jules Ginswick, *Labour and the Poor in England and Wales 1849-1851*, Vol III, (1983).
W. K. V. Gale, *Ironworking*, (1981).

Acknowledgements

First published in 1989 by the Merthyr Tydfil Heritage Trust

ISBN 1 871404 04 5

Permission to reproduce illustrations has been given by the following:
David Anderson page 27.
Sir William Crawshay 12.
Cyfarthfa Castle Museum 7, 10, 11, 13, 16, 18, 24, 26, 32, 33, 36, 37, 38, 39.
Dowlais Library 19.
National Library of Wales, Aberystwyth 13.
National Museum of Wales, Cardiff 17.
Ron Price 34.
Tate Gallery 6.
Welsh Industrial and Maritime Museum cover, 5, 9, 25.

Photographs on pages 28, 29 are copyright Merthyr Tydfil Heritage Trust.

The Merthyr Tydfil Heritage Trust would also like to thank the Prince of Wales Committee, Jane Hodge Foundation, Mid Glamorgan County Council, and the Peter Nathan Charitable Trust for grants towards the publication of this book.